D1459748

HOW WE BUILD

BRIDGES

BRIDGES

Neil Ardley

GEC GARRETT EDUCATIONAL CORPORATION

Edited by Rebecca Stefoff

U.S.A. text © 1990 by Garrett Educational Corporation
First Published in the United States in 1990 by
Garrett Educational Corporation, 130 East 13th Street,
Ada, OK 74820

First Published 1989 by Macmillan Children's Books,
England, © Macmillan Publishers Limited 1989

Manufactured in the United States of America

Library of Congress Cataloging-in-Publication Data

Ardley, Neil.
    Bridges / Neil Ardley.
    p.   cm. - (How we build)
    Includes index.
    Summary: Describes various types of bridges and how they are built
and maintained.
    ISBN 0-944483-74-7
    1. Bridges-Juvenile literature. [1. Bridges.] I. Title. II. Series.
TG148.A73   1990
624'.2-dc20   90-40247
                                                                  CIP
                                                                   AC

Note to the reader
In this book there are some words in the text which are printed in **bold** type.
This shows that the word is listed in the glossary on page 46. The glossary
gives a brief explanation of words that may be new to you.

Contents

Over land and water

Everyone builds bridges. You may have made a sand bridge on the beach, or laid a plank across a stream so that you could walk across it. However, only people well skilled at putting scientific ideas into practice can build the ever longer and larger bridges needed today.

Engineers are constantly working to develop new and safer ways of putting up all kinds of structures using all types of materials. They can build skyscrapers standing over a hundred stories high. Huge oil rigs, strong enough to withstand the stormiest winds and waves, are anchored out at sea. Bridges are a common feature of our landscape, so engineers face the challenge of making them beautiful as well as useful.

▲ Bridges may be built to allow major roads to pass over each other without the traffic lanes meeting. This tangle of concrete near Birmingham, in England, carries roads on six levels.

◄ The Golden Gate Bridge crosses San Francisco Bay, in California. It is one of the most beautiful bridges in the United States, and was completed in 1937. It has a total length of 6473 feet (1973 meters).

How we use bridges

By crossing natural barriers like rivers and ravines, bridges make our journeys shorter and easier. By lifting roads above the streets of busy cities, they help to ease the traffic flow.

This is true whether the traffic consists of vehicles or pedestrians. Footbridges, or **overpasses,** allow people to walk over busy roads or railways safely. Sometimes bridges are built to allow farm animals and tractors to cross a road between a farm and its fields safely, without holding up the traffic. Bridges may be constructed to carry oil or water pipes, and even canals, over roads or railways.

Bridge building

Have you ever looked closely at a bridge? Have you ever wondered how bridges are built and what holds them up? Engineers plan each new bridge very carefully. They work out exactly how strong the bridge needs to be in order to carry the load it is expected to bear. Some bridges may also have to stand up to high winds, floods, or earthquakes. In this book you will read about the various ways in which engineers have tackled the problems of bridge building.

Long ago

The oldest bridges in the world were not made by people at all. They are natural arches of rock. Some of them were formed over the ages by rivers that bored their way through the rocks blocking their path. Others were created by wind, rain, or sandstorms that ate away at the softer rock and left the harder rock behind in the form of an arch.

When people first built bridges, many thousands of years ago, they laid tree trunks across narrow rivers and walked across them to reach the other side. In some places, ropes could be made by braiding vines and creepers together. When the ropes were slung between the river banks, they made a type of bridge.

Simple bridges like these eventually rot or get washed away, but people in many parts of the world still use bridges like them today. They are easily made from materials that are close at hand.

People in ancient times also crossed shallow rivers by moving big stones into place and stepping from one to another. Sometimes they laid large, flat boulders on top of the stones to form a bridge. This kind of bridge is called a **clapper bridge.**

Skilled engineers

It was not until about 5000 years ago that people learned how to build bridges over deep rivers. Historians have found evidence of a bridge built over the Nile River by the Egyptians about 4500 years ago. They think that it was probably built in the shape of an arch. The shape was important because **arch bridges** are very strong structures. The Babylonians, Greeks, Romans, and Chinese also knew

▲ Natural sandstone arches like this one in the Utah National Park in the United States were formed by the action of the wind on the soft rock.

▼ This stone clapper bridge crosses a stream on Dartmoor, in England. It is thought to be about 2000 years old.

how to build arches. The An-Chi Bridge at Chao Chou in China was built with the use of arches in about AD 600 and is still in use.

The Romans were very skilled engineers. They built roads, dams, and **aqueducts.** You can still see these ancient structures in many parts of Europe today. The Romans discovered how to build strong supports for their bridges in the river bed. The Pont du Gard in France is an aqueduct that shows how the Romans achieved this strength. The stone arches are built on three levels and spaced so that each level is supported by the one beneath it.

▲ The Pont du Gard, near Nîmes in France. The aqueduct was built by the Romans in AD 14 to carry water from the Gard River to the city of Nîmes, 25 miles (40 kilometers) away.

Bridges with houses on top

The period of the Middle Ages lasted from about AD 500 to AD 1450. During this time, people built stone arch bridges as the Romans had done. Most of these bridges were built across rivers that ran through cities. Often buildings were built along the tops of these bridges. There were houses, shops, churches, and even jails on some of them.

▼ The Ponte Vecchio is an arch bridge that was built during the Middle Ages in Florence, Italy. There are still shops on the bridge that sell gold and silver items to the many people who cross the bridge every day.

New methods and materials

From about 1600 onward, engineers were developing a new way of building bridges. They already knew how to join wooden beams together in a series of triangles to support the roofs of houses. Bridge builders used the same kind of supports, called **trusses,** to hold up bridges. They often built covers over these bridges to keep out the rain and protect the wooden trusses.

Metal bridges

During the 1700s, bridge builders also began to make use of new materials, particularly metals. They found that the strength of iron made it suitable for bridge building. Also, iron was easier to build bridges with than stone because it could be molded into different shapes.

Bridges were built by joining beams of iron called **girders** together. Long bridges could be supported by a truss made of criss-crossing girders. A road ran either across the top of the truss or inside the structure of the truss itself. Later, in the early 1800s, such bridges would carry the new railways.

By then, a process had been developed that could combine iron with small amounts of other substances to make steel. Steel was much stronger than the iron from which it was made. Steel proved to be ideal for bridge building. Engineers used girders and flat sheets, or plates, of steel to construct much bigger bridges than before. The first large steel arch bridge was built in 1874 across the Mississippi River in the United States.

▼ The world's first bridge made from iron was built in 1779 at Ironbridge, in England. It still stands today.

▲ The Clifton Suspension Bridge in England was completed in 1864. It stands 240 feet (73 meters) above the Avon River and is 692 feet (211 meters) in length.

▼ Switzerland's Salginatobel Bridge was completed in 1930. It is supported by a graceful concrete arch of great strength.

Hanging bridges

The lightness of iron and steel soon made it possible for engineers to suspend their bridges in the air between two towers. These **suspension bridges** can cross very wide stretches of water. On the first such bridges, built in the early 1800s, the roadway hung from iron chains. Later builders used long strands of steel twisted together into cables. In 1883, the Brooklyn Bridge became the first suspension bridge to be built with steel cables. It was erected in New York City.

Concrete bridges

About a hundred years ago, engineers began to use a mixture of cement, sand, stones, and water for their bridges. These concrete structures could be molded into whatever shape was needed. Steel rods placed inside the concrete give it added strength. This is called **reinforced concrete.** Since 1900, many thin and curved bridges have been built from reinforced concrete. Some of them are very beautiful.

Types of bridge

There are three main types of bridge: **beam bridges,** arch bridges, and suspension bridges. Beam bridges are very common. You see them often above major roads and railways. Arch bridges are built to allow traffic to travel beneath them. A suspension bridge can be built high above waterways to allow large ships to pass under the bridge. However, each of the three main types of bridge depends on a different kind of support.

Supported by the land

A short beam bridge rests on solid ground at each end. A plank laid across a ditch is a very simple form of beam bridge. The weight of the bridge presses down on the supporting land. The beams or girders of the bridge must be very strong, so that the bridge does not bend in the middle.

A longer beam bridge may rest on river banks or cliffs, or on tall columns that rest on the river bed or valley floor between. These columns, or **piers,** hold up the bridge. The part of a bridge between two supports or two piers is called a **span.** Very long beam bridges, like those crossing wide rivers or those built to take rail traffic, have many spans.

Two or three parts

One type of long beam bridge is made up of two sections, each of which has its main support at one end. This is a **cantilever bridge.** The supports at each end of a cantilever bridge mean that these bridges can be used to cover greater distances than simple beam bridges. There is no support for the middle of a

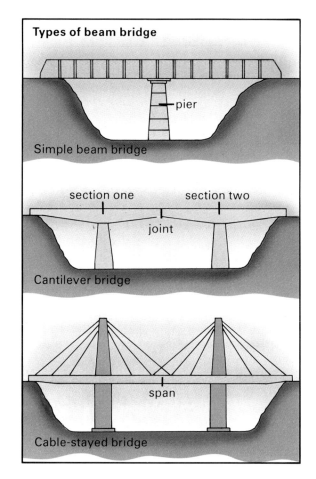

Types of beam bridge

pier

Simple beam bridge

section one   section two

joint

Cantilever bridge

span

Cable-stayed bridge

cantilever bridge. Instead, each of the two sections of the bridge rests on the land at one end and on a single pier at the center of the section. The rest of each section sticks out and is joined to the other section at the middle of the bridge by a single beam. Sometimes cantilever bridges have a third section in the middle, to make the bridge longer.

Towers and cables

Some beam bridges have high towers above the piers. Cables extend from the tops of the towers to the bridge beam. They help to strengthen the bridge and hold it steady. This is a **cable-stayed bridge.**

Testing a beam bridge

You will need: a sheet of cardboard such as part of a cereal box, four books, some light and heavy objects such as toy cars, trains, trucks, or cans of food.

1 Cut an oblong strip of cardboard from the box about 12 inches (30 centimeters) long and 3 inches (7 centimeters) wide. Draw dotted lines on the strip as shown, about 2 inches (5 centimeters) from each end.

2 Rest the cardboard strip on two of the books, lining up the dotted lines as shown. Place the objects on the span one by one until it collapses. How much weight can the bridge support?

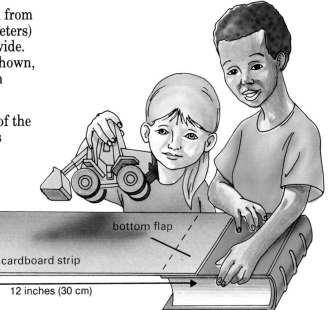

top flap

2 inches (5 cm)

3 inches (7cm)

bottom flap

cardboard strip

12 inches (30 cm)

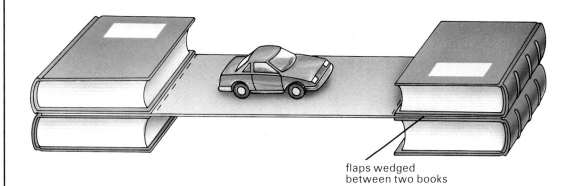

flaps wedged between two books

3 Now put the beam bridge together again. Lay the other two books on the two ends as shown. Repeat the tests. Is the bridge stronger now?

Save the materials for your next project, on page 14.

Curved supports

Arch bridges and suspension bridges both have curved supports. These supports make these types of bridges very strong.

Arch bridges

An arch bridge does not rest on the land at each end, like a beam bridge, and it has no piers to hold it up. Instead, the two ends of the arch are anchored firmly into the ground at each end of the bridge and the bridge curves upwards towards the middle.

Sometimes a road or path follows the curve of the arch. However, such a slope may slow down traffic and prevent drivers from seeing what is ahead of them. More often, a straight roadway is built above the arch. In some arch bridges, the road or railway passes below two large arches, from which it is suspended.

Make an arch bridge

You will need: the strip of cardboard, books, and the same light and heavy objects that you used for the project on page 13.

1 Bend the strip of cardboard to make an arch bridge like the one shown.

2 Now find out how much weight your bridge can support. Place the objects on it, one by one, until it collapses. Is the arch bridge weaker or stronger than the beam bridge?

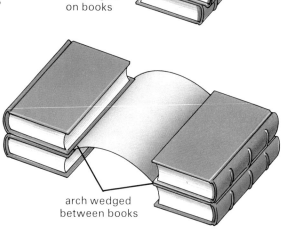

cardboard strip

arch lodged on books

3 Fold the strip along the dotted lines as shown. Wedge the flaps under the top book on each side to keep them firm. Push the books towards each other so that the cardboard bends into an arch.

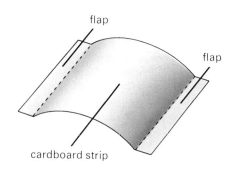

flap

flap

cardboard strip

arch wedged between books

4 Repeat step two of the project. Is the bridge weaker or stronger now?

Suspension bridges

A suspension bridge hangs from two sets of immensely strong steel cables. The cables curve downward from tall towers built on piers near each end of the bridge. Steel ropes attached to the cables hold up the girders that support the roadway. The cables pass over the tops of the towers and are fixed firmly to the ground at each end of the bridge.

Because the cables are strong enough to carry the whole weight of the bridge, there is no need for heavy supporting columns of arches. Even when the central spans are very long, the strength of the steel allows them to support the weight of the spans without difficulty. Suspension bridges have the longest single spans of all bridges. However, they are not practical for use as railway bridges, because trains are much heavier than cars and trucks.

Combination bridges

Some long bridges are built of two or more types of bridge. For example, the Chesapeake Bay Bridge in the United States is 17.3 miles (28 kilometers) long. It is made up of beam sections, cantilever sections, and suspension sections, and it includes two tunnels that join different parts of the bridge together.

▼ The Sydney Harbour Bridge, in Australia, carries a wide roadway between huge steel arches. The bridge was opened in 1932.

▼ The Varrazano Narrows Bridge, in New York, is a long suspension bridge completed in 1964. Its main span is 4258 feet (1298 meters) long.

15

Planning a bridge

Before the builders can start to construct a bridge, a lot of planning has to be done. First, the government, or whoever plans to have the bridge built, must decide if the benefits of the new bridge will justify the cost and the disruption caused by the construction. They must find out if it is really needed. How many people will use it? Will they have to improve the roads leading to and from the bridge?

The site

Next, the site of the bridge must be chosen and the land must be bought. This can take a long time if the land is being lived on or farmed. Finally, the bridge builders can start work.

Surveyors measure the land. Deep holes are bored into the ground to take samples of the soil and rock. The builders have to find out if the rock is hard enough to act as a support for the bridge. If it is not, a base of reinforced concrete will have to be built for the bridge to stand on.

If the bridge is to cross a river, the builders take samples from the river bed for testing. They also measure the force and volume of the water in the river. The bridge supports must not be weakened by floods. They find out all they can about wind speeds and weather conditions in the area. The bridge may have to withstand storms, blizzards, or even hurricanes.

When the bridge builders have collected all the information they need, the **architects** can begin to design the bridge. Their plans will show in detail how the bridge is to be built and how it will look when it is finished.

▲ A surveyor must make detailed measurements of the site before a bridge can be built.

Choosing the type of bridge

The builders choose the type of bridge most suitable for the particular site and for the bridge's intended use. Will it carry pipelines, or road or rail traffic? Will it cross a road, railway, river, or valley? How long will it need to be? What will look best in the setting chosen for it? The answers to these questions will determine the type of bridge that is built.

Strength tests

Before the bridge is built, it is important to know the **forces** that will act on it. Engineers estimate the weight of each part of the bridge and the pressures that the parts will exert on each other. They predict the weight of the traffic that the bridge will carry and allow for accidents that could shake its structure. The bridge must be able to withstand the forces of water, wind, and earthquakes.

The engineers use computers to work out all the forces that will affect the finished structure, and also the building costs. Then they make an exact scale model of the bridge and test it to make sure that the bridge they have designed will be safe under all conditions.

▼ The wind resistance of this model bridge is being tested in a wind tunnel. Engineers need to make sure that the design of the bridge will be strong enough to withstand the worst weather conditions.

Building materials

While the architects are designing a bridge, the builders decide what materials to use. Wood, stone, and iron are rarely used any more. The builders will probably choose steel or concrete.

Most new bridges, especially traffic bridges, are built of concrete. The advantage of concrete is that it does not need much care after it is built. The disadvantage is that it is very heavy. Long spans can only be built of steel, which is much lighter. However, most steel bridges get rusty unless they are painted regularly. If no one is prepared to pay the continuing costs of painting, the builders must choose a kind of steel that does not rust.

Many bridges contain both steel and concrete. Concrete bridges are usually strengthened inside with steel, and steel bridges usually carry a concrete roadway.

Building in steel

The steel plates and girders used in bridge building are manufactured to the exact size and shape needed by the builders.

Plates and girders may be joined by large metal pins or **rivets** that pass through holes in the sections to be joined, gripping them tightly together. Or they may be joined edge to edge by **welding.** The welder works with an **oxyacetylene burner,** which burns hot gases. Its flame melts the steel where the plates or girders meet, and the edges flow together. When the steel cools, it sets and makes a smooth, hard join.

▲ A welder wearing a protective mask and clothing uses an oxyacetylene burner to weld rivets into place.

Building in concrete

Concrete sections can be made in any shape the builders choose, by pouring liquid concrete into molds and allowing it to harden. The sections can be fixed together with bolts or with a powerful glue.

Concrete by itself is hard, but it is not very strong. To strengthen concrete, engineers run steel rods through it, creating reinforced concrete. Sometimes a framework of steel rods, or wire mesh, holds the concrete together.

Often the steel rods are first stretched, or **stressed,** and then covered with liquid concrete. The rods squeeze the concrete, making it strong, so that it does not crack easily. Concrete sections made in this way are said to be **pre-stressed.** Sometimes concrete is poured into molds with holes, or ducts, through them. After the concrete has set steel rods are pushed through the holes and then stretched. The concrete is said to be **post-stressed.**

▲ A concrete beam will begin to bend when heavily loaded.

▲ The base of the beam starts to crack where the concrete is pulled apart.

▲ Placing a steel rod inside the beam holds the concrete together and stops the beam from cracking.

▲ Stretching the rod and then releasing it to squeeze the concrete makes the beam very strong.

A firm base

Some of the most important parts of a bridge cannot be seen. They are hidden underground. These are the bridge's foundations, which are rooted deep in the ground or river bed. They hold the structure firmly so that it cannot move. If a bridge lacks solid foundations, it is likely to collapse.

Solid supports

Bridge builders start their work by putting down the foundations. The first foundations must support the concrete or stone structures that join the bridge to the land at either end. These are the **abutments.** The builders begin to prepare for these by digging large holes in the ground.

If the ground is firm, the builders then fill the holes with concrete to form huge slabs. The abutments are built on top of the concrete slabs.

If the ground is soft, even concrete slabs may not provide firm foundations for the abutments. The workers must first drive long rods or beams, called **piles,** deep into the ground. The piles are usually made of steel or concrete, and they are hammered into the ground by large machines called pile drivers. The concrete slabs that are then built on top of the piles are firm enough to support the abutments.

▶ The type of foundations that will be built to support abutments depend on whether the building site is on firm or soft ground.

Abutment foundations

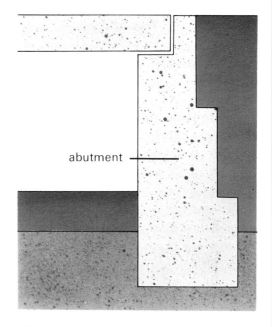

abutment

▲ The foundations of the abutment are built underground in hard rock.

▲ The abutment is supported by foundations made of reinforced concrete.

Pier foundations

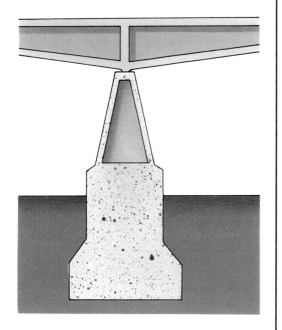

▲ The base of the pier is set in a mass of solid concrete.

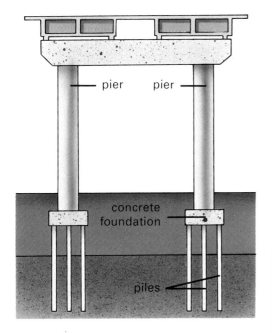

pier   pier

concrete foundation

piles

▲ The foundations of the pier are strengthened by long piles that are driven deep into the ground.

▲ A pile driver is a machine like a huge hammer. It drops a heavy weight on to the pile and drives it into the ground.

Piers

Many bridges are supported by piers, which also need firm foundations. Concrete slabs are laid, as for the abutments, and the piers are raised on top of them. The piers may be built of concrete or steel. They may be in the form of one thick column or a group of slender columns. Often, the pier itself is a narrow column with a large base and a wide top to carry the road or railway track.

The piers beneath a bridge must be extremely strong. They support the weight of the bridge and must remain standing through floods, earthquakes, landslides, or any other disasters that might occur.

Building bridges in water

When a bridge is built across a river, the piers will stand in the water. This means that their foundations will probably need to be supported by piles. How can the river bed be kept dry while the construction work is going on? Engineers have solved this problem in various ways.

Sunken dams

One way is to build a temporary dam, or **cofferdam,** where the pier is to go. The bridge builders sink long beams of concrete, steel, or wood into the river bed to make a square or circular wall that rises above the water level. They then pump out all the water from inside the cofferdam, so that work can be carried out on the river bed. They may dig down through the mud and soil until they reach

Build a cofferdam

You will need: modeling clay, a drinking straw, a plastic or paper cup with the bottom cut out, and a sink.

1 Flatten out a ball of modeling clay so that it is wider than the bottom end of the cup and about one half-inch or one centimeter thick.

2 Stick the clay onto the bottom of the sink. Fill the sink to the depth of the cup.

3 Press the cup into the clay so that it sticks firmly, with the open end up.

4 Suck all the water out of the cup with the straw and spit it out. You have made a miniature cofferdam.

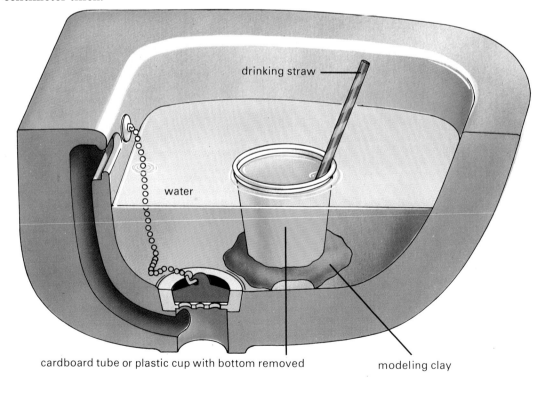

drinking straw

water

cardboard tube or plastic cup with bottom removed

modeling clay

▲ Working on a river bridge poses many problems. A cofferdam can be used to seal off a part of the river bed while the piers are being built.

▲ A caisson in position at the building site. It is a watertight box or tube which allows the workers to dig down into the river bed. The caisson will be filled with concrete to form part of the permanent bridge foundations.

hard rock. They may sink piles into the ground. Concrete can then be poured into the hole to make a foundation for the pier.

When the foundations are ready, the construction workers build the pier on top of them. When the pier has risen above the top of the cofferdam, the cofferdam is taken apart and may be used again.

The construction workers do not always work inside the cofferdam. Sometimes, instead of pumping out the water, they use floating cranes to dig out the mud and soil.

Giant boxes

If the water is deep, engineers use a huge container, called a **caisson,** instead of a cofferdam. The caisson is floated out into position in the river. Some caissons are simply filled with concrete and sunk to the river bed, so that the concrete in the caisson forms the foundations for the bridge's pier.

Other caissons are open-ended. After the caisson is set on the river bed, the water is pumped out of it to make a watertight space for construction work. Cranes remove the mud and soil from inside the caisson until they reach bedrock, or pile drivers sink the necessary piles. The caisson is then pumped full of concrete to form the pier's foundations.

Concrete arch bridges

You may have seen an arch bridge spanning a broad river or a valley in a single, graceful curve. The bridge does not need piers to hold it up. The arch alone has the strength to do that.

Starting construction

The ends of an arch bridge need very firm foundations, because they support the whole weight of the bridge. You have already seen how builders construct abutment foundations at each end of a bridge before they build anything else. The abutments for a concrete arch bridge form large, sloping blocks that jut out from the land on each side. These blocks are called **skewbacks.**

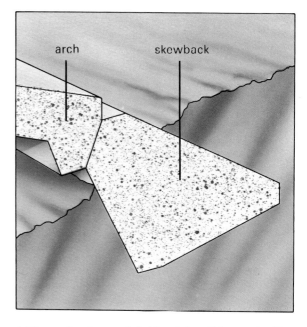

▲ The ends of an arch bridge take all the strain. The skewback must be part of a very strong abutment.

▼ The Gladesville Bridge, in Sydney, Australia, during construction. The arch sections were placed across a supporting framework.

Raising an arch

Some arch bridges are made of steel. They are built by joining steel girders together so that they grow out from each end to meet in the middle.

However, most arch bridges are made of concrete and need something to hold them up as they are built. The builders make a large supporting framework of wood or steel in the shape of the arch. It is built across the full width of the valley or river, but may have openings for road or river traffic to pass through.

The arch itself is constructed out of specially shaped, hollow concrete blocks. Large numbers of these are made elsewhere and brought to the building site by truck. There, cranes lift each block into its position on the frame.

Several layers of concrete blocks, called **ribs,** are positioned side by side to form the complete arch. Once the blocks are in position, concrete is poured between them to fix them together. Each rib is built in two halves that start at the skewback and meet in the middle.

When the arch is finished, the framework can be taken down. The pressure from the two abutments out to the center of the arch will prevent it from falling. Columns graduated in length can be built on top of the arch to support the road or railway that will go across it.

▼ The finished Gladesville Bridge, with the frame removed from the arch. Raised columns support the roadway.

Upper structures

The first stages of building a beam or arch bridge include the construction of the foundations, abutments, piers, and arches. Work on the upper structure can begin only when these supports are in place. The top part of the bridge that carries the road or railway is known as the **deck.**

In a short bridge, without piers or arches, the deck rests on the abutments. In longer bridges, the deck is carried on piers or a single arch. A very long bridge may use a series of piers or arches to carry the deck. Suspension bridges, however, are different, as their decks are supported from above.

Bending and twisting

The deck of a bridge is usually made of the same materials as the supports. It has to be strong so that it remains flat and does not bend between its supports.

The deck carries large, heavy, moving vehicles like trucks and trains. The weight is uneven. As the vehicles move along the surface of the deck, they press down on the structure in different places. Strong winds may blow against the deck. Together, the forces of the wind and the weight of its load could twist the deck out of shape. To avoid disaster, the deck of a bridge must be rigid.

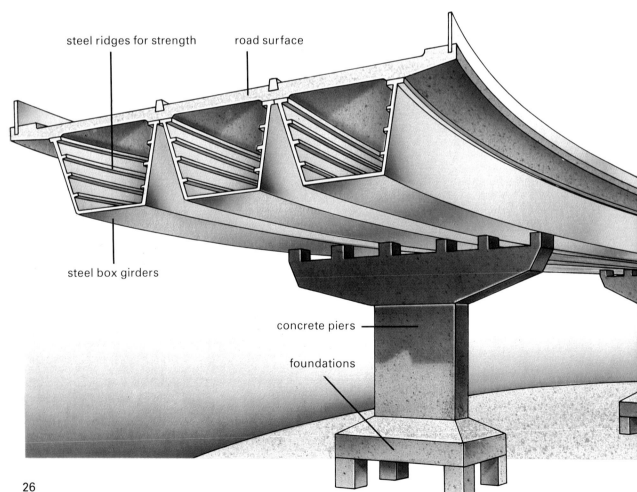

steel ridges for strength

road surface

steel box girders

concrete piers

foundations

▼ The deck of a road bridge is supported by strong steel box girders.

▲ The old Britannia Railway Bridge, built across the Menai Straits, in Wales, between 1845 and 1850, was an early box girder bridge. Trains ran through rigid iron boxes.

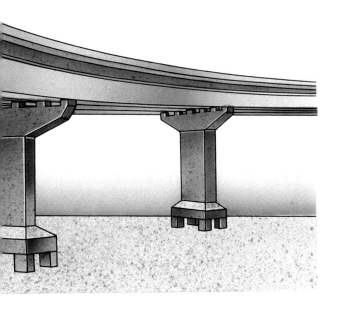

Girders for strength

To prevent the deck from twisting or bending, strong girders are placed across the bridge's support below the road or railway. These girders are beams of steel or concrete.

Girders can be made in the shape of long, hollow boxes of steel or concrete. These **box girders** rest on the supports, and also serve as the deck for the road or railway. Box girders are light, because they are hollow, but they are also very strong and stiff.

Building the deck

The deck can be added to the supports of a bridge in several ways. The method chosen depends upon the nature of the site where the bridge is being built. Sometimes the builders can work from below and raise the deck into position. Often they have to build the deck high in the air.

Frames and cranes

The decks of bridges that cross over roads are often built on top of a wide supporting framework made of wood or steel. The box girders, or other deck sections, are made elsewhere and then brought to the site.

Construction workers use cranes to hoist the girders or sections into position and then join them together. When the deck is finished, the builders dismantle and remove the frame.

Making a frame for a very high bridge, or a bridge across water, may be either too difficult or too costly. In these situations, the deck of the bridge can be made elsewhere and brought to the site on trucks or barges. Cranes then lift the deck up into position on the supports, and workers attach it to the supports. Usually the deck is raised in short sections that are then joined together.

▼ The deck of this bridge is being built across a supporting framework of steel girders.

Bridges that grow

Sometimes it is impossible to bring cranes to the site. The ground below the bridge may be too rough or slope too steeply. Alternatively, construction barges would be dangerous moored in the middle of busy shipping routes on rivers and lakes.

In such cases, bridge builders have to construct the deck by working from the top of the supports. Usually the workers build the deck outward from one support to the next. They attach a short section of the deck to the top of each support and then, working on that, join further sections to it. The bridge grows slowly outward from the supports until it all meets in the middle.

▲ Cranes may be used to raise sections of deck into position.

▼ A deck takes shape. Concrete sections extend outwards from the piers.

Starting a suspension bridge

Suspension bridges are among the most impressive structures in the world today. Some of them are huge, crossing rivers that are more than a mile (two kilometers) wide and having towers that are more that 490 feet (150 meters high). The central span between the towers may be three times as long as the longest single span of any other kind of bridge.

Anchoring the cables

However large a suspension bridge may be, its tall, slender towers, gently curving cables, and ribbon-like roadways make it look very graceful. From a distance, it looks almost delicate. Yet suspension bridges are very strong.

A suspension bridge needs very firm foundations. Work begins when a deep shaft is bored into hard rock on either side of the river. If there is no hard rock, enormous holes are dug in the ground. The shafts or holes are then filled with concrete, which is strengthened with long steel rods.

The cables of the bridge will be fixed to the rods, so that the cables are anchored to the ground by the concrete blocks. The blocks can withstand immense pressure. Each cable can pull on the blocks with a force of 10,000 tons or more without moving them. These blocks hold up the bridge.

The towers

The towers of the bridge are built next. The base of each tower is constructed in the water, inside a cofferdam or caisson. The work is done in the same way as for the piers of a beam bridge, but these foundations must be even stronger, to support the great weight of the towers.

The towers themselves may be built by bolting steel plates together to form two slender steel columns, or they may be built of concrete. At the top of each tower, the bridge builders place a steel block, called a **saddle,** over which the cables will run.

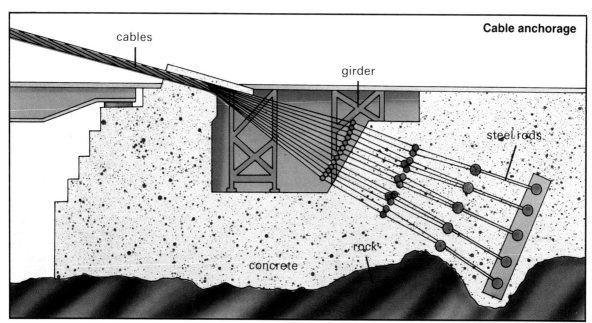

Cable anchorage

cables

girder

steel rods

rock

concrete

▲ Workers fit the saddle to a tower of the Humber Bridge. The main cables run over the saddle.

▲ Work began on England's Humber Estuary Bridge in 1972. Towers were raised to a height of 535 feet (163 meters). When the bridge was opened in 1981, the towers supported the world's longest main span.

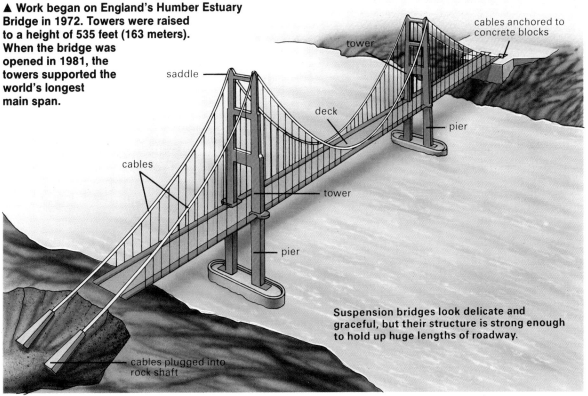

cables anchored to concrete blocks

tower

saddle

deck

pier

cables

tower

pier

cables plugged into rock shaft

Suspension bridges look delicate and graceful, but their structure is strong enough to hold up huge lengths of roadway.

Completing a suspension bridge

Once the foundations of the suspension bridge and the towers are built, the cables are placed in position. If they are brought to the site ready-made, they are hauled or towed across the river and lifted onto the towers by cranes. However, the cables for many long bridges are made on the bridge itself, high up in the air, in their final position.

Cable making

The workers start by slinging huge steel ropes from tower to tower to connect the two banks of the river. From these ropes a walkway, or **catwalk**, is hung for the use of construction workers.

The cables are then made from thousands of thin but strong steel wires. The wires are taken back and forth along a continuous wire rope above the catwalk

▲ High on the catwalk, a worker reels in steel wire off the wheel. The main cables for a suspension bridge are spun from strands of steel wire.

on a wheel, which feeds out the wires. The construction workers bundle the wires together to form the cables. **Hydraulic squeezers** press them tightly and wrap them in more wire for protection.

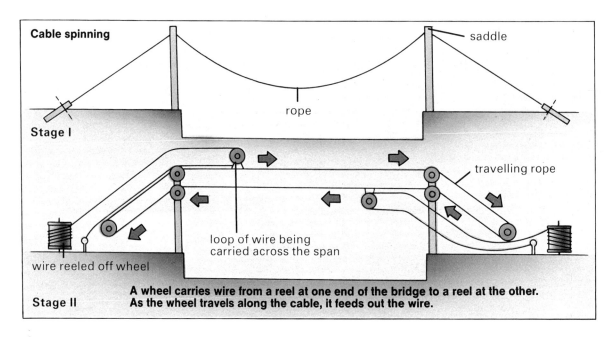

Cable spinning

saddle

rope

Stage I

travelling rope

loop of wire being carried across the span

wire reeled off wheel

A wheel carries wire from a reel at one end of the bridge to a reel at the other. As the wheel travels along the cable, it feeds out the wire.

Stage II

Fitting the deck

The deck of the bridge hangs from the suspension cables, so the next step is to place the **hangers** in position. These are long lengths of wire rope that hang vertically from the suspension cables. They are fixed to the deck by strong steel clamps.

The deck is made elsewhere and brought to the bridge in short sections. Barges carry the deck sections out on the river until they are beneath the waiting hangers. Cranes hoist the sections into the air, where workers attach them to the hangers and join them together.

The deck is made of steel, so it is light. Girders may be placed along the sides of the deck to make it rigid. Or the deck itself may take the form of a shallow box girder. The suspension cables and hangers that support the deck are not rigid. Without the girders, the deck might twist or swing in the wind. The deck may also be made narrower at each end to reduce the force of the wind blowing against it.

Build a suspension bridge

You will need: studded building blocks, about six feet (two meters) of yarn, three pairs of rubber bands in three sizes, and sticky tape.

1 Use the blocks to build two towers like the ones shown.

3 Space the rubber bands along the yarn, with the largest size at the tower ends and the smallest size in the middle. Fix them to the yarn with the tape.

4 Join a number of long bricks to make a deck. Push the deck through the rubber bands to make the bridge shown below.

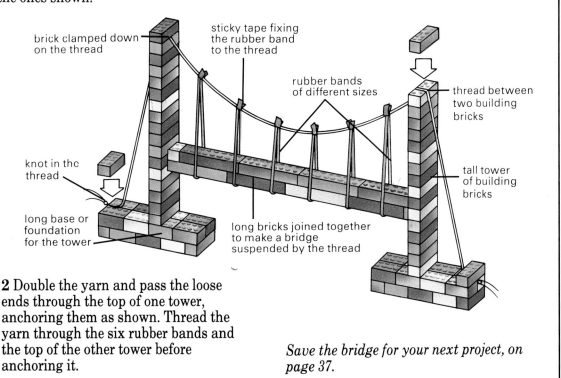

brick clamped down on the thread

sticky tape fixing the rubber band to the thread

rubber bands of different sizes

thread between two building bricks

knot in the thread

tall tower of building bricks

long base or foundation for the tower

long bricks joined together to make a bridge suspended by the thread

2 Double the yarn and pass the loose ends through the top of one tower, anchoring them as shown. Thread the yarn through the six rubber bands and the top of the other tower before anchoring it.

Save the bridge for your next project, on page 37.

Care and safety

In hot weather, a bridge expands slightly. In cold weather, the bridge contracts slightly. These changes can weaken the bridge, because they either squeeze or stretch the deck. To avoid this, the bridge has a hidden part that makes it safe at all times. It is called an **expansion joint.** One or more of these joints are built into the deck of the bridge when it is made. An expansion joint gives the sections of the deck room to move as they change size. The movement prevents damage to the deck from occurring in hot or cold weather.

The bridge builders have not finished when the deck of the bridge is in place. Whatever the type of bridge, there is still more work to do. They have to lay the road surface or railway tracks on the deck. They must construct the drains to carry away rainwater. The whole structure may need painting. Then they install the guard rails, signs, and traffic lights that make the bridge safe to use.

The opening of a new bridge is an important occasion. It costs a great deal of money to build. Many people have been involved in the planning and building. Guests are invited to the opening ceremony and a band plays as some famous person or government official declares the new bridge open.

▼ Princess Anne opening the Erskine Bridge in Scotland, in 1971. The bridge spans the Clyde River.

Painting and inspection

Once the bridge is open, the whole structure has to be checked and maintained so that it stays in good condition.

Unless it is built of non-rusting girders, a steel bridge is usually painted. The paint keeps the steel from getting rusty, which would weaken the structure. One coat of paint is not enough, however. The repainting of big steel bridges like the Forth Rail Bridge, in Scotland, never stops.

Concrete bridges do not rust and are not painted. However, all types of bridges are inspected regularly to make sure they are safe. Inspectors use hanging platforms called **cradles** to reach all parts of the structure. The cradles may be slung from the piers, towers, or deck. They permit a close look at cracks and any other signs of weakness in the bridge. If the inspectors find anything wrong, repairs must be done immediately.

Traffic control

The flow of traffic across the bridge may be controlled from stations at each end. On a long suspension bridge, only a certain number of vehicles can safely be allowed on the bridge at any one time. Severe weather conditions, like fog, ice, or high winds, will limit the number further. The bridge may even have to be closed to traffic at times.

▼ Welders carry out essential repair work. It is vital that bridges are kept in good condition and that any necessary repairs are made to them.

▼ The movement of vehicles across the Forth Road Bridge in Scotland is monitored in the toll station control room. Drivers pay a toll to cross the bridge. The money collected helps to finance repairs to the bridge.

Bridge failures

When builders construct a bridge, they make it as safe as they can. However, accidents sometimes happen, and bridges sometimes fail. They may have hidden weaknesses, or be subjected to unforeseen shocks. The supports may give way when a ship crashes into them or they may collapse when an earthquake strikes.

Bridge builders today know a great deal about the materials they use and the forces that act on the bridge. If there is a failure, it usually happens while the bridge is being built. It might be caused by weak links between sections, which fail before the bridge has been completed.

It is very unlikely that a bridge will fall down when it is in use, no matter what happens to it. However, there have been some terrible disasters in the past.

▲ When the Tay Bridge was blown down, the engineer who built it admitted that he had failed to allow for wind forces when he designed the bridge.

▼ Wind was also the cause of the collapse of the Tacoma Narrows Bridge in 1940. The wind set off a shaking motion that broke up the bridge.

The Tay Bridge Disaster

One of the worst bridge disasters in history happened in Scotland in 1879. A rail bridge had been built over the Tay River the previous year. It was huge, nearly two miles (three kilometers) long. During a very stormy night, the central span collapsed as a train was crossing it. The train plunged into the river, and 75 people were killed.

The Tay Bridge was a steel beam bridge, with trusses of girders supported on piers. Strong winds were the immediate cause of the bridge's failure, but the steel trusses may have been badly built.

The Tacoma Narrows failure

High winds were also the cause of the collapse of a huge suspension bridge at Tacoma Narrows, Washington, in the United States in 1940. The bridge was the third longest bridge in the world and it had only been open four months. First it began to heave up and down in the wind, then it began to twist, until at last it broke into pieces. Luckily, the people on the bridge had time to get off before it collapsed.

Learning from failures

Engineers can learn from bridge failures. The Forth Rail Bridge in Scotland, a huge cantilever bridge, was built soon after the Tay Bridge disaster. The builders made ample allowances for strong winds in the Forth River, and the bridge is still standing a hundred years later.

After the Tacoma Narrows failure, bridge builders found out how to make the deck of a suspension bridge stiff enough to withstand strong winds. No such failure has happened since.

Test a suspension bridge

You will need: the suspension bridge you made on page 33, toy cars, and a hair dryer.

1 Use the hair dryer to blow air at the bridge. Blow air from the top, from the sides, and from under the bridge. Can you make the bridge sway? Can you make it fall down?

2 Rebuild it, if necessary, and put some toy cars on the bridge. Test its strength again. What difference do the cars make?

3 Try any ways you can think of to make your bridge stronger in the wind.

Safety first: Treat electrical appliances with care and common sense. Never use a hair dryer near water.

hair dryer blowing air

Bridges that move

The people who design and build beam bridges, arch bridges, and suspension bridges make sure that their bridges will stand firm and not move. Any movement of the structure could cause it to fail.

However, there are bridges that are designed to move. These are low bridges built over a river or harbor that is used by ships and boats. The bridges must be built with decks which can move out of the way to let shipping through.

People and traffic must get off a moving deck of a bridge before it moves. Barriers close the roads that lead to the bridge.

Tilting bridges

The drawbridges of old castles were raised and lowered by simple machinery, to stop enemies from crossing the castle moat. They were an early form of **bascule bridge.** Today, bascule bridges are operated by an electric motor at one end of the deck. The deck is raised to allow ships to pass up and down the river, and lowered to allow cars to cross it. When the bridge is lowered, it rests on a support on the far side of the river.

A double bascule bridge has two deck sections, both of which tilt upward when they are raised. The two sections meet in the middle of the river and lock together when the bridge is lowered.

▼ London's famous Tower Bridge has double bascules which can be raised to allow river traffic to pass along the Thames River.

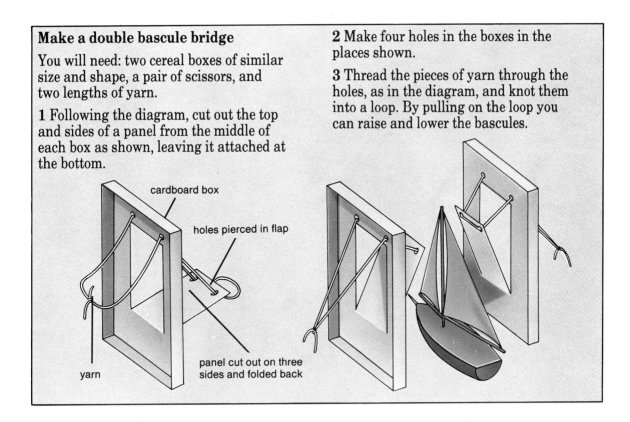

Make a double bascule bridge

You will need: two cereal boxes of similar size and shape, a pair of scissors, and two lengths of yarn.

1 Following the diagram, cut out the top and sides of a panel from the middle of each box as shown, leaving it attached at the bottom.

cardboard box

holes pierced in flap

yarn

panel cut out on three sides and folded back

2 Make four holes in the boxes in the places shown.

3 Thread the pieces of yarn through the holes, as in the diagram, and knot them into a loop. By pulling on the loop you can raise and lower the bascules.

Rising bridges

A **lift bridge** acts just like an elevator. The whole deck rises in the air when a ship or boat has to pass. There are two high towers at the ends of the bridge. Cables in the towers support the bridge. These cables lift the bridge up and let it down. Electric motors in the towers or on the bridge drive the cables.

Turning bridges

Some bridges turn through a right angle to get out of the way of ships and boats. A **swing bridge** usually rests on a pier in the river, though some swing bridges turn on piers at the shore. After the ship has gone through, the bridge is swung back, so that it joins up with the road on each bank.

▲ This lift bridge spans the St. Lawrence River at Montreal in Canada. The whole span can be raised by the piers at either side.

Floating bridges

A bridge is not always raised up above the water. Sometimes bridges are built on the surface of the water itself.

Armies on the move need to be able to build bridges quickly in order to cross rivers as they come to them. They carry special sections of roadway made to float on water. These bridges are simply laid in place and tied to the banks. After the river has been crossed, the army collects the sections of the bridge together, loads them onto trucks, and moves on.

Crossing the Hellespont

In ancient times, armies sometimes tied boats together to cross a stretch of water. In 481 BC, Xerxes, king of Persia, built a famous floating bridge out of 674 vessels

---

Make a floating bridge

You will need: three plastic food containers, a bath, modeling clay, scissors, a sheet of cardboard, some toy cars and a drinking straw.

1 Fill the bath with enough water to float the three containers. They are the pontoons.

2 Roll some clay into short ropes. Use them to anchor the pontoons to the edges of the bath as shown.

3 Cut the cardboard into strips the width of the pontoons and lay a roadway across the pontoons.

4 Prove that the bridge works by driving the toy cars across.

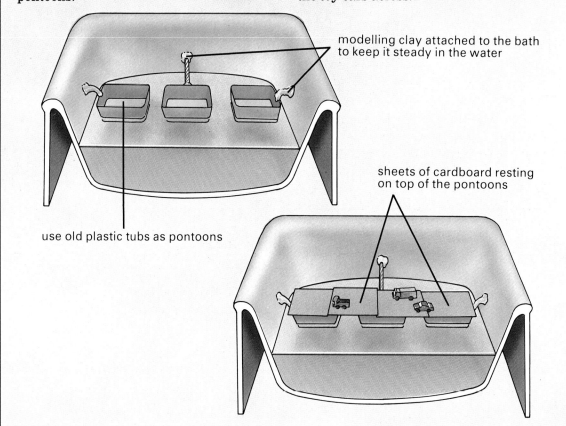

modelling clay attached to the bath to keep it steady in the water

use old plastic tubs as pontoons

sheets of cardboard resting on top of the pontoons

across the Hellespont, a strait of water now called the Dardanelles between European and Asian Turkey.

The ships were tied together by ropes and firmly anchored to the bottom of the channel. Then a roadway of logs was built across the boats. The Persian army, with its horses and chariots, crossed this great floating bridge to invade the continent of Europe—but the army was later defeated by the Greeks.

Permanent floating bridges

Some floating bridges are built to stay in place permanently, usually because the soil on the site is too soft to support a fixed bridge. However, such a bridge will only remain safe if the water it crosses is very calm.

There are several large floating bridges on Lake Washington, near Seattle, in the United States. They are called **pontoon bridges.** The pontoons are hollow blocks of concrete that float in the water. The bridges are made of several pontoons bolted together. Each pontoon is anchored by cables to heavy concrete blocks buried in the bed of the lake. The road runs along the top of the pontoons.

Floating bridges often have a gap between the pontoons halfway across, so that ships and boats can pass through. The roadway normally bridges the gap, but it can slide back onto the pontoons when necessary.

Bridges of the future

Wherever people build new roads and railways, they need to construct bridges. If you think about it, even airports are full of overpasses built to keep passenger, road, and rail traffic apart and flowing smoothly.

As road and rail traffic reaches further and moves faster than ever before, more bridges than ever will be needed. Bridges save time and shorten distances. In many cases, they save money, too. However, how much longer and larger can bridges get?

Non-stop travel

Cars can go faster than most people dare drive them, and new high-speed trains can reach speeds of 125 miles (200 kilometers) an hour. However, both roads and railways come to a stop when they reach water. Islands are still islands.

Countries, and even continents, may be separated by only a narrow channel of water, but it can take hours to get across it by ferry.

The English Channel, between Britain and France, will soon be crossed by a tunnel instead of by a bridge, since no one has yet designed a bridge that will cross the 20 miles (32 kilometers) that separate the two countries. However, there are plans to build a huge suspension bridge across the Strait of Messina, linking the island of Sicily to the mainland of Italy. The central span of this bridge would be about two miles (three kilometers) long. It would have towers 234 feet (300 meters) high.

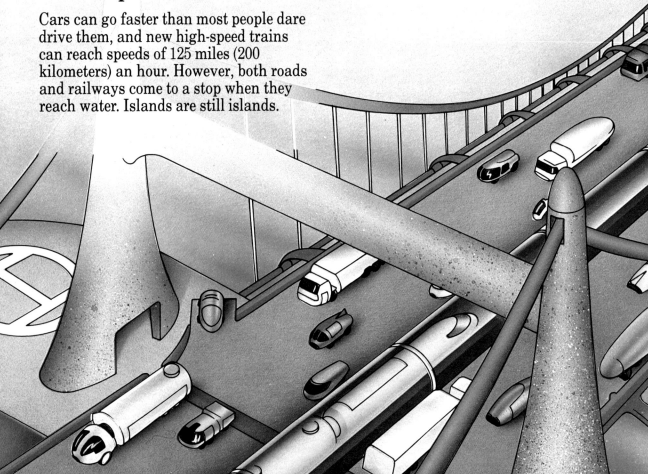

New materials

New materials keep being developed that could be useful to bridge builders. They include special kinds of plastics, which are reinforced in the same way as concrete is. These materials are both light and strong. Plastic bridges could be built with longer spans than bridges have now.

In the future, people may drive from Europe to Africa across the Strait of Gibraltar, on a bridge more than nine miles (15 kilometers) long.

Did you know?

* The longest bridge in the world is the Second Lake Pontchartrain Causeway, which is more than 23 miles (38 kilometers) long. It is in Louisiana, in the United States. The bridge is built of concrete spans, each of which is 56 feet (17 meters) long. It was completed in 1969, and is so long that no land is visible from the middle of the bridge.

* The longest single span in the world is the 4626-foot (1410 meter) main span of the Humber Bridge, a suspension bridge which crosses the Humber Estuary in Yorkshire. It was opened in 1981.

    The Akashi-Kaikyo Bridge is currently being planned. It will link the islands of Honshu and Shikoku in Japan. Its main span will be 5840 feet (1780 meters) long.

* The bridge with the longest cantilever span is the Québec Bridge, over the St. Lawrence River in Canada. The bridge was completed in 1917. The length of the main span between the piers is 1801 feet (549 meters). The cantilevers are constructed of steel trusses.

* The world's longest arch bridge is the New River Gorge Bridge in West Virginia, in the United States. It is a steel arch bridge with a span of 1700 feet (518 meters).

* The longest concrete arch bridge is the Brotonne Bridge over the Seine River in France. It has a span of 1050 feet (320 meters) and was completed in 1977.

* The longest floating bridge is the Second Lake Washington Bridge in Seattle, Washington, in the United States, completed in 1963. The floating section of the bridge is 1.5 miles (2.4 kilometers) long.

* The world's highest bridge is a suspension bridge over the Arkansas River in Colorado, in the United States. The deck is 1053 feet (321 meters) above the water. The bridge was completed in 1929.

* The widest bridge in the world is the Crawford Street Bridge in Providence, Rhode Island, in the United States. It is 1148 feet (350 meters) wide.

* The widest long-span bridge is the Sydney Harbour Bridge, a steel arch bridge in Sydney, Australia. The deck is 161 feet (49 meters) wide over a span of 1670 feet (509 meters). It carries two railway tracks, eight traffic lanes, a cycle path, and pavement.

▼ The Great Seto Bridge links the islands of Honshu and Shikoku in Japan. It was opened on April 10, 1988, after taking ten years to build. It is the longest dual-purpose bridge in the world, carrying both cars and trains on different levels. Now the journey by car across the bridge takes ten minutes compared to one hour by ferry. The bridge is formed by a series of six spans and viaducts and is 8 miles (12.8 kilometers) long. The six spans have been designed to withstand the most powerful typhoons and earthquakes.

Glossary

abutment: a part of a structure that is designed to withstand the force or weight of the part next to it.

aqueduct: a structure, often a bridge, built to carry flowing water from place to place.

arch bridge: a bridge in which the spans are built in the form of a supporting curve.

architect: a person who designs and oversees the building of a structure.

bascule bridge: a bridge in which a section of the roadway can be raised at an angle.

beam bridge: a flat, rigid bridge that is supported at each end.

box girder: a long beam of steel or concrete made in the shape of a box for extra strength.

cable-stayed bridge: a kind of beam bridge which is strengthened by cables attached to the deck from a central tower.

caisson: a watertight box inside which builders can work on river beds.

cantilever bridge: a type of beam bridge made up of two or more sections. Each section is supported by the bank at one end and by a central pier.

catwalk: a high, narrow, pathway for work on the cables of a suspension bridge.

clapper bridge: an ancient type of bridge built over a stream.

cofferdam: an enclosed barrier that keeps part of a site dry enough to work on while a bridge is being built over a river.

cradle: a movable platform that hangs on cables down the side of a bridge.

deck: the section of a bridge that carries the path, road, or railway.

engineer: a person who makes use of scientific ideas in order to build structures, mines, or machines, or to work with chemicals or electricity.

expansion joint: a joint in a structure that allows each section to shrink or grow in size as the temperature changes.

force: the strength or power affecting an object.

girder: a long metal beam used for strength and support in large structures such as bridges and skyscrapers.

hangers: vertical lengths of steel rope that hang from suspension cables to hold up the deck of a suspension bridge.

hydraulic squeezer: a machine that presses metals or other objects together.

lift bridge: a bridge whose deck can be raised temporarily.

overpass: a section of main road raised to pass over other roads or railways.

oxyacetylene burner: a tool that is used for joining or cutting steel. It burns a mixture of the gases oxygen and acetylene.

pier: a pillar that is built beneath a bridge as a support.

pile: a beam made of concrete, steel, or wood. Builders drive piles deep into the ground in order to provide a firm support for a bridge.

pontoon bridge: a river or sea bridge that is supported by a series of boats or floats.

post-stressed concrete: concrete that is strengthened by stretched steel rods inserted after the mixture has hardened.

pre-stressed concrete: concrete that has been poured over stretched steel rods.

reinforced concrete: concrete that has been poured over a framework of steel rods.

rib: one of the layers of concrete blocks that forms a complete arch in bridge building.

rivet: a metal bolt or pin used to fasten metal plates together.

saddle: a steel block at the top of a suspension bridge tower that supports the bridge's main cables.

skewback: the projecting side support for a concrete arch bridge.

span: the section of a bridge between two supports.

stress: to stretch a rod of steel.

suspension bridge: a bridge in which the roadway is hung from steel cables supported by towers.

swing bridge: a bridge that can be swung to one side to allow ships to pass.

truss: a framework of beams built to support a structure.

welding: joining two pieces of metal.

Index